Contents

KU-527-569

Any words appearing in the text in bold, **like this**, are explained in the glossary.

What is a volcano?

A volcano is a hole in the Earth's surface. The hole reaches down into a pool of hot, liquid rock below. Most of the time, a volcano is silent and still. However, it can also suddenly **erupt**. When it erupts, boiling rock from inside the Earth spurts out of the opening. This **lava** may spill out like bubbling treacle, or it may shoot into the air at high speed. Some volcanoes give off clouds of **ash** and gas as well.

Incredible power

Most of the volcanic eruptions that happen are small, but some can cause terrible destruction. They can damage buildings, injure, and kill people. A large, violent, volcanic eruption can destroy all life for kilometres around.

Why are they called volcanoes?

The Romans named a volcanic island 'Vulcano', after their god of fire, Vulcan. Gradually the name came to mean all volcanoes.

This is red-hot lava pouring out of the Soufrière Hills volcano, on the Caribbean island of Montserrat, in January 1997.

AWESOME FORCES OF NATURE

VIOLENT VOLCANOES

Revised and updated

Louise and Richard Spilsbury

www.raintreepublishers.co.uk
Visit our website to find out
more information about
Raintree books.

To order:
☏ Phone 0845 6044371
📠 Fax +44 (0) 1865 312263
🖳 Email myorders@capstonepub.co.uk

Customers from outside the UK please telephone +44 1865 312262

Edited by Megan Cotugno, Abby Colich, and Andrew Farrow
Designed by Richard Parker
Original illustrations © Capstone Global Library 2004
Illustrated by Geoff Ward
Picture research by Hannah Taylor
Production by Alison Parsons
Originated by Capstone Global Library Ltd
Printed and bound in China by Leo Paper Products Ltd

ISBN 978 0 431178 75 2 (hardback)
14 13 12 11 10
10 9 8 7 6 5 4 3 2 1

ISBN 978 0 431178 82 0 (paperback)
14 13 12 11 10
10 9 8 7 6 5 4 3 2 1

British Library Cataloguing in Publication Data
Spilsbury, Louise.
   Violent volcanoes. -- 2nd ed. -- (Awesome forces of nature)
   1. Volcanoes--Juvenile literature.
   I. Title II. Series III. Spilsbury, Richard, 1963-
   551.2'1-dc22

Acknowledgements
We would like to thank the following for permission to
reproduce photographs: Corbis: **9** (Frans Lanting), **18** (Jeremy
Horner); Getty Images: **4** (Kevin West), **8** (Three Lions/Evans),
21 (AFP Photo/Bay Ismoyo), **23** (John T. Barr), **24** (AFP
Photo/Romeo Gacad), **26** (AFP/ Romeo Gacad); Istockphoto:
15 (Koch Valérie); NASA: **25** (GSFC/METI/ERSDAC/JAROS
and U.S./Japan ASTER Science Team); Photolibrary: **10** (Ron
Dahlquist), **13** (Joe Carini), **17** (Paul Lawrence); Reuters
27; Rex Features: **16** (Sipa Press), **19** (Sipa Press), **20** (Sipa
Press/Christophe Colombie); Science Photo Library: **14**
(Explorer/Krafft), **22** (Prof. Stewart Lowther); Shutterstock: **28**
(Jeff Banke); Still Pictures: **5** (Peter Arnold, Inc./Otto Hahn),
11 (Kevin Aitkens).

Cover photograph of hot ash flow from Mount Merapi,
Indonesia in 2006 reproduced with permission of Photoshot
(UPPA/ WpN).

We would like to thank Dr. Ramesh Srivastava for his
invaluable help in the preparation of this book.

Over millions of years, ash and lava from eruptions can build up to form mountains like Mount Etna in Italy.

Volcanoes can completely change the way the land around them looks. They can blast away patches of ground and create new areas, such as hills or slopes. Some volcanoes shoot so much ash into the sky that they change the weather in an area for months on end.

Volcanic mountains

Most volcanoes are shaped like mountains. This is because the lava sets hard when it cools down in the air. Over time volcanoes may erupt many times. This slowly builds the volcano up into a mountain that is shaped like a cone.

VOLCANO FACTS

❶ Between 50 and 70 volcanoes erupt every year across the world.

❷ More than a million people have been killed by volcanic eruptions in the last 2000 years.

❸ There are more than 1000 volcanoes on land that could erupt at some time in the future.

❹ **Molten** rock inside the volcano is called **magma**. When it erupts it is called lava.

What causes volcanoes?

Volcanoes are places where the red-hot **magma** from deep inside the Earth reaches the surface. To understand how this happens, you need to know a bit about how our planet is made.

What is the Earth like?

If you think of the Earth as a giant egg, we live on the shell, the outer surface. This outer layer is called the **crust**. Although the crust feels deep and solid to us, it is really quite thin compared to the size of the planet. Beneath this hard, cool surface lies hot, liquid rock.

This magma moves, rising and sinking very slowly. Long ago these movements made cracks in rock beneath the Earth's crust. This rock is actually split into seven huge pieces and several smaller pieces called **plates**. The crust and plates form the land we live on and the floor of the oceans. Although we cannot feel them moving, the plates are floating on the hot, liquid rock beneath them.

The Earth's surface is made up of enormous plates of rock. They fit together like the panels on a football.

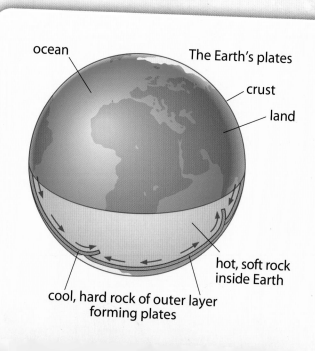

ocean

The Earth's plates

crust

land

hot, soft rock inside Earth

cool, hard rock of outer layer forming plates

How does a volcano form?

Volcanoes form when some of the hot, liquid rock squeezes through gaps between the plates. The magma forces its way up. As it rises, it melts rock that gets in its way, making a tunnel all the way through the crust.

Near the top, it gets stuck. More and more hot rock rises. Over many years, the amount of hot rock pushing on the crust gradually builds up. Suddenly there is so much that it bursts through the crust – the volcano **erupts**. It is rather like the way that a bottle of fizzy drink suddenly sprays out when you open the lid after shaking it.

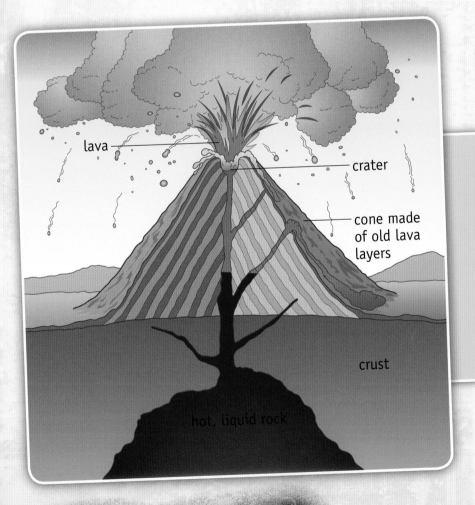

lava

crater

cone made of old lava layers

crust

hot, liquid rock

This picture shows you how a volcano works. Hot liquid rock pushes up from below the surface of the Earth to the top. The top of the volcano is called the **crater**. The sides are called the **cone**.

Volcano's on land

After an **eruption**, **lava** cools down and sets into hard rock. **Ash** settles on the ground like grey snow. A volcano may erupt several times. Each time, it gets a bit taller as more lava sets and more ash settles. When lava is very thick it runs downhill slowly. This makes a mountain with steep sides. When lava is thin it runs down fast and spreads out more. This kind of lava forms a wider, flatter mountain.

Ash pours from Mount Parìcutin in Mexico in 1950. The volcano erupted for nine years, from 1943 until 1952. When it was finished, only one building in the village of San Juan, Mexico remained standing.

Volcanoes in the sea

Most volcanoes actually happen underwater, on the **ocean floor**. They erupt and grow just as they do on land. Each time these volcanoes erupt, they grow a little larger. Some underwater volcanoes grow so tall that their tips stick out above the water. They form islands in the sea. In some places, a whole line of undersea volcanoes has created a chain of islands.

Hot spots

Some volcanoes form far away from the edges of the Earth's **plates**. These volcanoes form over points in the Earth called **hot spots**. These are places in the Earth's surface where the liquid rock is so hot that it pierces a hole through a weak point in the **crust**.

This is a picture of the volcano caldera that has grown above water on Isabela Island in the Galapagos Islands. It is an example of an underwater volcano that has grown so tall that it sticks out above the water.

CASE STUDY

Hawaiian islands

The islands of Hawaii are actually the tips of underwater volcanoes. These volcanoes have built up over many thousands of years to become huge mountains. They are so tall that they show above the water as islands.

Each volcano is formed from **lava** that bubbled up from the same **hot spot** in the Earth's **crust**. The hot spot stays in the same place all the time. However, the floor of the Pacific Ocean is part of a **plate** that is moving very slowly. As one volcano moves away from the hot spot it dies. Then a new one begins to form above the hot spot. This has created a string of volcanoes, like beads on a necklace. One, Mauna Kea, in Hawaii, measures over 9500 metres from the **ocean floor** to its peak. It is taller than Mount Everest!

HAWAIIAN ISLANDS

PACIFIC OCEAN

This aerial photograph of an Hawaiian island was taken from an aeroplane. The islands are actually the tops of giant volcanic mountains that begin deep beneath the ocean.

Where do volcanoes happen?

There are lots of volcanoes all over the Earth, on land and on the ocean floor. Most volcanoes are deep under the sea. This is partly because the crust that forms the ocean floor is thinner than the crust that forms the land we live on. The hot, bubbling rock can rise up through the thin ocean floor more easily.

Where plates meet

More volcanoes happen on the ocean floor because that is where the edges of the world's plates meet. Most volcanoes happen where plates meet because this is where the hot liquid rock from inside the Earth can break through and rise to the surface.

This photo shows volcanic bubbles emerging from the top of a reef under the ocean.

Ring of Fire

More than half of the world's volcanoes are found around the edges of the Pacific Ocean where **plates** meet. This is also where most of the world's **earthquakes** happen. This area is called the 'Ring of Fire' because so many fiery, volcanic explosions happen there.

However, volcanoes do not only happen where plates meet. Volcanoes can also sometimes occur in the middle of plates. There are also volcanoes in places where plates are slowly pulling apart, such as Surtsey near Iceland.

This map shows you where the active volcanoes of the world today are located. You can see that most of them lie around the Ring of Fire in the Pacific Ocean. They affect countries such as Japan, Indonesia, and many other islands.

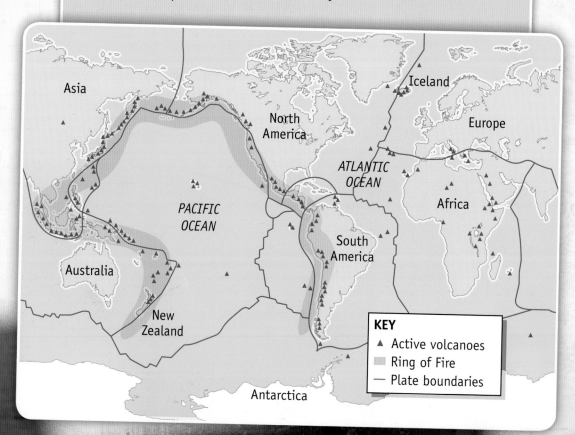

Asia

North America

Iceland

Europe

ATLANTIC OCEAN

Africa

PACIFIC OCEAN

South America

Australia

New Zealand

Antarctica

KEY
▲ Active volcanoes
▨ Ring of Fire
— Plate boundaries

When do volcanoes erupt?

Small volcanoes **erupt** more often than big volcanoes. This is because it takes a very long time for a large amount of liquid rock to build up to cause a big volcanic eruption. Some smaller volcanoes may have a gentle eruption every few months. However, there is no way of telling exactly when a volcano will erupt.

What are active and dormant volcanoes?

Across the world there are more than 1000 **active** volcanoes. This means that they have erupted within the last 2500 years and may erupt again soon. **Dormant** volcanoes are those that have not erupted for a very long time. Sometimes volcanoes remain dormant for many years but then erupt suddenly.

This is Mauna Loa in Hawaii. It usually erupts every 3 or 4 years. Sometimes it can erupt again after just a few months or remain dormant for as long as 25 years.

What happens when a volcano erupts?

Some volcanoes **erupt** gently. The **lava** spills out slowly. Gases and steam rise off the lava and form small clouds above the volcano. Other volcanoes seem to explode. These violent eruptions usually cause the most damage.

When a volcano erupts, broken rock and **ash** often spurt out with the lava. They may be thrown straight up into the air like burning clouds above the volcano. Then they pour down like a fountain. The huge chunks of volcanic rock can drop down to Earth like heavy bombs. The most dangerous eruptions happen when mixtures of hot ash, rocks, and gases rush down the side of a volcano at high speed. Speeding flows like this can burn everyone and everything in their path.

In some eruptions lava can shoot high into the air above the volcano. It looks like a fiery fountain.

What does lava do?

When lava is runny, it can pour down the side of a mountain very fast. It can also spread a long way. Some lava has streamed hundreds of kilometres away from the volcano it first came out of.

When lava is very thick, it does not move so quickly. It moves slowly enough for people to get out of its way. As lava flows over land and streets it knocks down and burns everything in its path. It flattens trees and other plants and spreads itself like a thick blanket over the land.

VOLCANO FACTS

❶ Lava can reach five times the temperature of the hottest pizza oven.

❷ A mixture of hot ash, rocks, and gases can travel down steep slopes at 200 kilometres an hour – that's as fast as a speeding sports car!

❸ A fountain of lava can shoot as high as 1500 metres into the air.

Nothing can stop a river of lava like this, as it spreads over the land.

What damage does ash do?

Ash is made up of bits of rock so small that they look like dust. The fine ash that comes out of some volcanoes can form massive clouds. Wind can spread the ash clouds over vast areas. These clouds can **pollute** the air. When the air is full of ash it causes breathing problems for people on the ground. It also makes it hard for people to see. In the past, this has caused road, train, and aeroplane accidents after a volcano.

Sometimes ash falls from the sky like grey snow. It can **choke** and burn people and cover and kill plants. It blocks rivers and streams and kills the fish that live there. It clogs telephone and radio systems and ruins machinery.

When tonnes of ash fall together, it can bury buildings. Ash can be very heavy, especially if it gets wet. It can collapse roofs.

Can volcanoes cause other natural disasters?

Some volcanic **eruptions** are so powerful that they also cause other natural disasters. For example, the heat of the **lava** can melt snow and ice on a volcanic mountain. When this water mixes with ash, the ash becomes like mud and slides down the mountain. This is called a mudflow and it can bury whole towns.

Volcanoes can also cause avalanches, landslides, and tsunamis. Avalanches are when large slabs of snow or ice slide down a mountain. These slide down the mountainside and cover anything in their path in deep snow. Landslides are like avalanches, but they are when mud, rock, and trees from a mountain tumble down onto homes and land below. When underwater volcanoes erupt they can create tsunamis. These are giant waves that can wash over coastlines and drown people and wreck buildings.

This huge crater in the snow was caused by an avalanche. The avalanche happened when a volcano erupted.

Can volcanoes be helpful?

We often hear about the destruction volcanoes cause. However, volcanoes are also important and useful to us. They have shaped the land all around us and they made the Earth a place where animals could live! Ancient volcanoes gave off steam that later became water, and gases that helped to form the air. These are things that all living things on Earth need to survive. Today in some countries, people trap steam that comes from volcanoes to produce electricity to heat and light towns and cities.

VOLCANO FACTS

❶ More than 80 per cent of the rock surface of the Earth was formed by volcanic **eruptions**. This includes the **ocean floor** and the mountains of the world.

After a volcano erupts, ash and **lava** fall onto soil and in small amounts can make it fertile. This means that **crops** grow very well on it. That is one reason why many farmers, like this one in Colombia, live and work on the slopes of volcanoes.

CASE STUDY

Colombia, South America, 1985

Nevado del Ruiz is a volcano in South America. It had been **dormant** for a long time, until it began sending out puffs of smoke in 1984. In spite of these hints that the volcano was waking up, people living nearby stayed. Then, suddenly, on 13 November 1985 there were two violent explosions.

The explosions threw millions of tonnes of **ash** into the air. As the hot ash fell to the ground, it melted ice and snow, creating a river of mud. It poured over the nearby town of Armero, burying people and buildings under 5 metres of mud. Then the muddy water grew into a deeper river over 16 metres deep. It destroyed several other villages in its path, before it finally stopped.

The rivers of mud caused by the Nevado del Ruiz volcano killed at least 22,500 people.

Who helps after a volcano?

Imagine the scene after a volcano. People's homes may be buried under **ash** or burned by hot gases and rocks. Burning rocks dropped from the sky may have set trees and buildings on fire. Roads and bridges may have been cut off by **lava** flows and the air may be thick with smoke.

The first to arrive in scenes like this are the emergency services. Firefighters brave the heat to put out fires where they can. They may also help army and rescue workers save people who are trapped in crushed buildings. Ambulance workers help to rescue burned or injured people. Then they transport patients to hospital. If the volcano has **erupted** without warning, people may need help **evacuating**.

Helicopter rescue teams may fly over an area to spot survivors after a volcano. They can lift them to safety without needing to land.

After the eruption

Volcanoes can erupt several times, so it may be a while before it is safe for people to return home. Once the area is safe, workers need to clear up **debris**. They check that buildings are safe. They rebuild ruined buildings, replant trees, and replace or resurface bridges and roads.

While all this is happening, people who have left their homes behind need somewhere to stay. **Aid organizations**, such as the Red Cross, set up **shelters** and provide people with bedding, food, drink, books, and games. Naturally, many people feel very upset after a disaster like a volcano. Some **aid** workers are specially trained to help people talk about their fears and feelings, to help them recover.

A woman registers in order to get relief goods from aid workers after the eruption of Mount Merapi in Indonesia in May 2006.

Mount St Helens, USA, 1980

Mount St Helens is a volcano in a **range** of mountains called the Cascades, in north-western, USA. In 1980, the volcano had been **dormant** for over 120 years, but it was about to awake. On 18 May it exploded violently, causing the worst volcanic disaster in the history of the USA.

One part of the volcano broke off and slid down the mountain, covering a vast area of land below. Millions of tonnes of **ash** and steam blasted down millions of trees. The ash and gases burned up any living things they met and started fires that raged for months. An avalanche of mud and rock knocked down trees, roads and entire hillsides.

> 66
>
> *'The mountain sounded like a giant cement mixer tumbling rock, popping, and banging with incredible volume and intensity.'*
>
> Lu Moore, a holidaymaker who survived the eruption
>
> 99

USA

• Seattle

WASHINGTON

▲ Mount St Helens

Some of the ash that exploded out of Mount St Helens formed a cloud 20 kilometres high.

Clearing up

The **eruption** transformed the beautiful wooded mountain area into a grey, dusty wilderness. The US Army Corps of Engineers removed nearly one million tonnes of ash from roads and airports. They dumped it into old quarries and planted grass on it, to stop the ash blowing away again. Every day for months, workers loaded and drove 600 lorries full of broken trees away. It cost over 1 billion US dollars to clear up the mess.

Ash from Mount St Helens covered roads, land and houses far around.

VOLCANO FACTS

❶ The eruption of Mount St Helens killed 57 people, including some who were 20 kilometres away.

❷ Thousands of animals, including deer, elk, and bear, were killed.

Can volcanoes be predicted?

It is very difficult to tell exactly when a volcano might **erupt**. Some erupt without any warning. However, scientists try to predict when volcanoes might erupt to give people time to **evacuate**.

When the ground moves

Before a volcano erupts, **magma** rises towards the surface. As it rises, it usually makes the ground nearby vibrate (move) slightly. Scientists measure the trembling of the ground with a special machine called a **seismograph**. Seismographs can pick up even tiny movements that could mean a volcanic eruption is on its way.

The seismograph draws a straight line on paper. When the ground moves, even a little, the line wiggles.

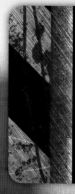

Mount Pinatubo, Philippines, 1991

Mount Pinatubo is a volcano on Luzon Island in the Philippines. When it erupted on 12 June 1991, around 800 people died. It could have been much worse. Scientists had predicted the eruption would happen and 60,000 people had evacuated in time!

Changing shape

The liquid magma that builds up under a volcano may make a bulge at its top or in its side. Sometimes a large patch of ground may rise by a few centimetres. This is another sign that liquid rock may be building up below ground. Scientists use machines called **tiltmeters** that show up any changes in the shape of the land like this.

Heat and steam

As magma rises to the surface, it often makes the land around the volcano much warmer. Scientists can take special photographs of volcanoes that show if there are any warm patches. Another sign of activity is steam coming from a volcano. When water inside the volcano is heated up it escapes into the air as steam.

This is a thermal image of Mount St Helens taken in March 2005, one week after a major **ash** and steam eruption. A new **lava** dome was created in the south-east part of the **crater**.

Can people prepare for volcanoes?

Volcanoes can kill and injure people and cause terrible destruction. However, if people and governments prepare properly, they can save lives and reduce the damage caused by volcanoes.

Working together

Scientists can prepare maps that show where **lava** or **ash** are likely to fall if a particular volcano **erupts**. They do this by studying the volcano and reports about eruptions that happened in the past. When towns grow up near a volcano, governments can use these maps to work out where the most dangerous areas are. Then they can build important buildings that hold many people, such as schools, hospitals, and **power plants**, away from danger areas. People can also strengthen buildings to cope with ash falling on their roofs.

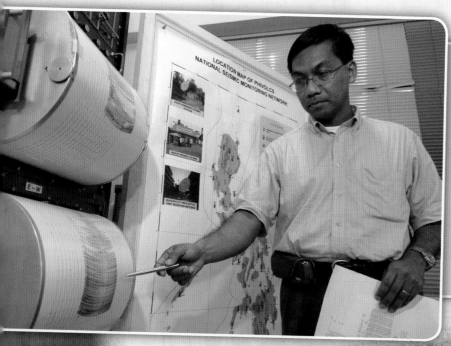

A scientist checks the recordings on a **seismograph**. It is important that volcano activity be monitored as closely as possible, so that governments have enough time to evacuate those areas that are in danger from an eruption.

This sign shows an emergency evacuation sign close to a volcano in Mexico. It tells people where they should go if there is an eruption.

Learn to be safe

Even if scientists can predict when a volcano will erupt, this will not be much help if people do not understand the dangers and the warnings. People need to learn how to prepare, what signs to look for, and how to listen to and obey warnings. If people have to **evacuate**, they have to follow instructions and do so as quickly as possible.

Disaster supply kit

Families living near a volcano should have a disaster kit ready. This should include:

- dried food and water
- a supply of clothes
- a radio, torch, and batteries for both
- goggles and breathing masks to stop people from breathing in ash
- pet food if needed
- a first-aid kit.

Can volcanoes be prevented?

Volcanoes are awesome forces of nature that cannot be stopped. Although they are a danger we can see, many people still live near them because the soil there is so good for farming. In the future we can hope that better prediction will help us know exactly when they will **erupt**. In the meantime, people who live near volcanoes should be safe if they listen for warnings and have properly worked-out disaster plans.

Do volcanoes ever die?

Volcanoes can 'live' for up to 1 million years, but they do eventually die. Sometimes a volcano dies when it blows itself up! When scientists believe that a volcano will never erupt again it is said to be **extinct**.

This is Crater Lake in Oregon, USA, located in an extinct volcano. Crater Lake formed from a high volcano that blew its own top off after a series of violent eruptions about 7700 years ago.

Violent volcanoes of the past

Krakatoa, Indonesia, 1883
This was one of the largest volcanic eruptions in history. The tsunami it caused killed 36,000 people. People more than 3000 kilometres away could hear the noise it made.

Mount Pelée, Martinque, 1902
This volcano on Martinique in the West Indies sprayed hot **ash** that set wooden ships in the harbour of the town of St Pierre on fire. About 29,000 people were killed by hot gases and ash moving at 160 kilometres per hour.

Novarupta, Alaska, USA, 1912
The largest US eruption released around 30 times more ash than Mount St Helens. Around 30 cm of ash fell in places 150 kilometres away.

Mount Bezymianny, Russia, 1956
This was one of the largest eruptions of the 20th century. Smaller eruptions started a year earlier. Luckily the volcano is a long way from any towns, so no one was killed. The amount of ash it sprayed out could have buried a large city!

Mount Agung, Bali, 1963
This volcano in south-east Asia killed about 1500 people, destroyed the homes of 85,000 others and ruined a third of the island's farmland.

Helgafell, Heimay, Iceland, 1973
The Helgafell volcano erupted suddenly and poured out tonnes of **lava** and ash. About 5300 people escaped from the island of Heimay in boats. The eruption lasted for over five months and covered vast areas of land in lava.

Nyiragongo, Zaire, Africa, 1977, 2002
Lava that flowed out suddenly from cracks in the side of the Nyiragongo **crater** killed around 100 people in 1977. It erupted again in 2002, killing over 100 people.

Mount Merapi, Sumatra, Indonesia, 1979
When this volcano erupted it poured rocks and lava onto villages nearby and killed 149 people.

Glossary

active word used to describe a volcano has erupted in the last 2500 years and may erupt again in the near future

aid help or assistance

aid organizations groups of people who work together to raise money and to provide help for people in need

ash volcanic ash is tiny jagged bits of rock. These bits of rock are so small they look like powder.

choke make it hard for an animal to breathe

cone sides of a volcano

crater the top of a volcano

crops food plants grown by farmers

crust hard surface of the land and the floor of the ocean

debris loose bits of solid material, such as stones and rock

dormant dormant means 'sleeping'. A dormant volcano is one that has not erupted for many years.

earthquake when the surface of the Earth moves

erupt/eruption when a volcano suddenly shoots out lava and ash

evacuate when people move from a dangerous place to somewhere safe

extinct word used to describe a volcano that scientists believe will never erupt again

hot spot place where hot, liquid (molten) rock pierces a hole through a weak point in the Earth's crust

lava red-hot liquid rock from inside the Earth, which spurts out of a volcano

magma melted rock

molten describes something very hot and melted

ocean floor rocky ground at the bottom of the oceans

plates the crust (the surface of the Earth) is divided into sections called plates

pollute to poison or harm any part of the water, land, or air in the world around us

power plant building where electricity is produced

range group of mountains formed at the same time and in the same way

satellite object that goes around the Earth in space. Satellites do jobs such as sending out TV signals or taking photographs.

seismograph machine that measures the shaking of the ground

shelter somewhere warm and safe to stay

tiltmeter tool that measures changes in the shape of the land

Find out more

Books

Landform Top Tens: The World's Most Amazing Volcanoes, Anna Claybourne (Raintree Publishers, 2009)

Mapping Earthforms: Volcanoes, Catherine Chambers and Nicholas Lapthorn (Heinemann Library, 2008)

Earth Erupts: Volcanoes, Carol Baldwin (Raintree Publishers, 2005)

Usborne Beginners: Volcanoes, Stephanie Turnbull (Usborne Publishing Ltd, 2007)

Disasters Up Close: Volcanoes, Michael and Mary Woods (Lerner, 2008)

National Geographic Readers: Volcanoes, Anne Schreiber (National Geographic Society, 2008)

Websites

www.howstuffworks.com/volcano.htm – the volcano pages of the How Stuff Works website will help you to find out more about how volcanoes work.

www.fema.gov/kids/volcano.htm – for facts about volcano dangers, what to do and how to prepare, visit the website of the US Federal Emergency Management Agency (FEMA).

www.volcanoworld.org – the Volcano World website has lots of great information about volcanoes, as well as some fun volcano games to play.

Index